Aunt Ruth Grammar Drills for Excellence I

A Workbook Companion to

I Laid an Egg on Aunt Ruth's Head

by

Joel Schnoor

Gennesaret Press
202 Persimmon Place
Apex, NC 27523

www.gennesaretpress.com

COPYRIGHT © 2017, 2018 Joel Schnoor. All rights reserved.

ISBN: 978-0-9845541-8-8

Printed in the United States of America
Apex, North Carolina

Front cover illustration by Doug Oglesby
Interior art by Ken High

Terms of Use: The following copyright privileges are granted for use of this document:

1. *Copies may be made of this document for use within one individual family.*

2. *For use in a classroom setting (public, private, middle school, high school, university, or home school cooperative), copies may be made for one classroom. Making copies for an entire school or school district is prohibited.*

3. *Other permissions may be obtained by writing Joel Schnoor at joel@joelschnoor.com.*

4. *This document may not be resold. Any media containing this document may not be resold.*

Table of Contents

Note: The "From Book Chapter (#)" column below corresponds with the chapter number in *I Laid an Egg on Aunt Ruth's Head* in which that particular topic was discussed.

Lesson	From Book Chapter (#)	Topic	Page
1	1	Lie / Lay (Part A)	7
2	1	Lie / Lay (Part B)	8
3	2	Hopefully (Part A)	9
4	2	Hopefully (Part B)	10
5	3	Little / Small	11
6	4	To Be and Pronouns	12
7	5	Aren't, Amn't, and Ain't	13
	6	Comprise	13
8		Review 1	14
9	7	Can / May	15
10	8	Further / Farther	16
	9	As / Like	16
11		Review 2	17
12		Review 3	18
13	10	That / Which	19
14	11	If I Were	20
15	12	Verbing / Verbizing	21
16	13	Everybody Is	22
17	14	Will / Shall	23
18	15	It's / Its	24
19		Review 4	25
20	16	Parentheses	26
21	17	Lose / Loose	27
22	18	Well / Good	28
23	19	Apostrophes	29
24	20	Real / Really	30
25	21	There / Their / They're	31

Lesson	From Book Chapter (#)	Topic	Page
26	22	You're / Your / Yours	32
27	23	Myriad	33
	23	Complimentary	33
	23	Stationery	33
28	24	Irregardless	34
29		Review 5	35
30	25	Capitalization	36
31	26	Split Infinitives	37
32	27	Dangling Participles	38
33	28	Whoever / Whomever	39
34	29	Using Past Participles	40
35	30	Many / Much	41
36	31	Between / Among	42
	31	Next / This	42
37	32	Principal / Principle	43
	32	Accept / Except	43
38		Review 6	44
39	33	Wake / Awaken	45
	33	E.g., I.e.	45
40	34	Dessert / Desert	46
	34	Literally / Figuratively	46
	34	Ensure / Insure	46
41	35	Alright / All right	47
	35	Alot / A lot	47
	36	Dropped Infinitives	47
42	37	Apostrophes in Names	48
	38	Advice / Advise	48
43		Review 7	49
44	39	Affect / Effect	50
	39	Unique	50
45	39	Comma Usage I	51
46	39	Comma Usage II	52
47	40	Nauseous / Nauseated	53
	41	Lead / Led	53

Lesson	From Book Chapter (#)	Topic	Page
48	42	Phenomena / Phenomenon	54
	42	Criteria / Criterion	54
	42	Data / Datum	54
	43	Historic / Historical	54
	43	Whether / If	54
49		Review 8	55
50		Comprehensive Review, Part 1	56
51		Comprehensive Review, Part 2	57
52		Comprehensive Review, Part 3	58
53		Comprehensive Review, Part 4	59
54		Comprehensive Review, Part 5	60
55		Comprehensive Review, Part 6	61
56		Comprehensive Review, Part 7	62
57		Comprehensive Review, Part 8	63
58		Comprehensive Review, Part 9	64
59		Comprehensive Review, Part 10	65
60		Comprehensive Review, Part 11	66
61		Comprehensive Review, Part 12	67
62		Comprehensive Review, Part 13	68
63		Comprehensive Review, Part 14	69
64		Comprehensive Review, Part 15	70

Lesson 1

Lie and Lay (Part A)

Use forms of lie to complete these sentences.

1. Aunt Ruth, thoroughly exhausted from her adventures, is going to _____ down and take a nap!

2. Yesterday, Binky _____ down and took a nap.

3. Lois has _____ down on the couch recently.

4. I was _____ in bed when you called me. I'm telling you the truth!

Use forms of lay or lie to complete the following sentences.

5. I was busy _____ the new sod in the back yard. I didn't notice that Aunt Ruth was _____ on a blanket, sunning herself. I'll dig her up tomorrow.

6. Last night, the chickens watched in amazement as Clovis _____ the book on the shelf.

7. He has no idea what he is doing. He has never _____ new carpet.

8. I need to _____ the egg on Aunt Ruth's head before she awakens.

Use the appropriate word to complete the sentence.

9. This worksheet is exhausting me. I need to _____ down a while and rest.

10. He _____ in bed all last week with the flu.

11. It's not polite to _____ on the couch when we have guests; you should be sitting!

12. She has _____ on the floor all day watching Aunt Ruth exercise!

Lesson 2

Lie and Lay (Part B)

Find the seven errors with lie and lay in the story below; write the corrections.

It was a dark and stormy afternoon, and Philbert was laying beneath the pecan tree. Next to him was his favorite hen, Rosie, who had lain four eggs that very day. I'm not lying.

Now, Philbert had laid beneath that tree before, and he had always enjoyed watching the squirrels scurry back and forth on the branches as they gathered nuts for dinner. On this particular afternoon, as he lied there with his eyes closed, he was listening to the sounds of the squirrels chattering. Rosie, too, seemed to be enjoying the squirrels as she worked on laying another egg. She had lay eggs there before and always enjoyed the furry little critters.

As he lay there, he began drifting off to sleep. He had a dream that a giant squirrel was climbing the tree, in search of the world's largest pecan. He imagined that the branches were creaking, twigs were snapping, and the tree was swaying under the weight of the huge squirrel.

Laying there, he was startled awake when he heard a clearly audible voice say, "I think I can, I think I can." He opened his eyes. Above him, perched in the tree, was Aunt Ruth! Carrying a bag of nuts and a bottle of glue, she was gluing the pecans onto the tree! Philbert watched her. She would glue a pecan and then eat a pecan; she would glue another pecan, and then she would eat another pecan.

"What are you doing, Aunt Ruth?" exclaimed Philbert. This startled Aunt Ruth, who hadn't seen him as he laid there below, and she lost her balance and fell out of the tree, landing right on top of Philbert and Rosie.

"Oh, you caught me," sighed Aunt Ruth. "I'm the Pecan Fairy, going around the world and gluing pecans onto all the pecan trees."

Rosie looked at Aunt Ruth, and then she clucked, "Are you nuts?"

Lesson 3

Hopefully (Part A)

Hint on Hopefully: Note that, in general, if you can substitute "I hope that" for "hopefully," then the "hopefully" is probably being used incorrectly.

Sentences that start out with "Hopefully, it will ..." are probably wrong, since "it" cannot be hopeful about anything.

"Hopefully, Aunt Ruth will arrive" does not mean the same thing as "I hope Aunt Ruth will arrive."

"Hopefully, Aunt Ruth will arrive" says Aunt Ruth will arrive in a hopeful manner. Why would she be hopeful? The speaker of the phrase most likely meant what is correctly stated in this phrase, "I hope Aunt Ruth will arrive."

Are the following sentences correct?

Example: Hopefully, it will rain tomorrow. No, this is not correct. It does not make sense that "it" will rain in a hopeful manner.

Example: Hopefully, I put a cake in the oven. Yes, this is correct. I was hoping the cake would turn out well when I put it in the oven.

1. Y / N   Hopefully, she won't forget about the party.

2. Y / N   Hopefully, Aunt Ruth stepped into the time machine.

3. Y / N   Hopefully, the mailman will be on time.

4. Y / N   Hopefully, I planned the surprise birthday party.

5. Y / N   Hopefully, this lesson on hopefully isn't too confusing.

6. Y / N   I hopefully auditioned for the symphony.

Lesson 4

Hopefully (Part B)

Example: Hopefully, we will enjoy the show. This is incorrect. We may have hopefully bought tickets (hoping we would enjoy the show), but if we enjoy the show, we probably would not do it in a hopeful way. We might do it in an appreciative or joyful way, though.

Use "Hopefully," or "I hope that" as appropriate.

1. _____ we will have a good snow this winter.

2. _____ the meeting will be a success.

3. _____ the little girl planted the carrot seed.

4. _____ I applied for the job.

5. _____ Aunt Ruth invited the nauseating nephew over for dinner (she was hopeful that he will behave himself).

6. _____ we will have a sunny afternoon for the picnic.

7. _____ the marching band will perform well.

8. _____ the marching band rehearsed.

(Note that some of these could use either choice, but one choice makes more sense than the other.)

Other adverbs can cause similar problems. Are these correct?

1. Y / N   Luckily, the frog landed in your soup and not in mine.

2. Y / N   Importantly, the invitation arrived today.

3. Y / N   Importantly, the little boy marched down the street with his tuba.

Lesson 5

Little and Small

Are these sentences correct?

1. Y / N   I am a small hungry this morning.

2. Y / N   I was a little tired last night.

3. Y / N   A small bird sat on the window sill.

4. Y / N   A little bird sat on the window sill.

Use little or small to complete the following sentences. If either will work, write "little / small" in the blank.

5. The papa bear was a _____ angry at Goldilocks.

6. The man was a _____ thirsty after being in the desert.

7. Could I have a _____ of your ice cream please?

8. I would also like a _____ piece of your rhubarb pie, please.

Are these sentences correct?

9. Y / N   I ate a little toast for breakfast.

10. Y / N   I was a small dismayed this morning when I awoke and found that Binky had eaten my breakfast.

11. Y / N   I drank a little milk for breakfast.

12. Y / N   I ate a small piece of toast.

13. Y / N   Can you play the tuba just a small more quietly please?

Lesson 6

Pronouns with To Be

Are these sentences correct?

1. Y / N   Hello, this is she.

2. Y / N   Hello, this is her.

3. Y / N   For whom is this gift intended?

4. Y / N   He thinks he is who?

5. Y / N   Yes, I am him.

6. Y / N   She gave cookies to Aunt Ruth and me.

7. Y / N   Us gave cookies to her.

8. Y / N   Those who have blue umbrellas are we.

9. Y / N   They hoped the blue umbrellas were sent to us.

10. Y / N   She gave cookies to us.

11. Y / N   She gave cookies to Aunt Ruth and I.

12. Y / N   Aunt Ruth and me gave cookies to her.

Use who or whom to complete the following sentences.

13. You are going to sing to _____ ?

14. To _____ are you going to sing ?

15. The next king will be _____ ?

16. _____ is going to give what to _____ ?

Lesson 7

Aren't and Comprise

Are these sentences acceptable generally in formal writing wherever English is used?

1. Y / N   I am not the king.

2. Y / N   I amn't the king.

3. Y / N   I are not the king.

4. Y / N   Aren't I the king?

5. Y / N   I ain't the king!

Are these sentences correct?

1. Y / N   Our zoo comprises apes and boars.

2. Y / N   The six of us comprise our family.

3. Y / N   Thousands of books comprise a library.

4. Y / N   The kingdom comprises many people.

5. Y / N   The ocean comprises many fish.

6. Y / N   Many adventures comprise Aunt Ruth's life.

Lesson 8

Review 1

Are the following sentences correct?

1. Y / N   He gave the possums to they and we.

2. Y / N   Madge gave the guacamole dip to we.

3. Y / N   Aunt Ruth modeled her new shoes for us and them.

4. Y / N   My uncle, Bill Grogan, served Clovis and I a goat dinner.

5. Y / N   Max gave Moby and I two cents each.

6. Y / N   Hopefully, she will bring the gizzards.

7. Y / N   I laid down for a nap this afternoon.

8. Y / N   Aren't you just a small curious?

9. Y / N   Ask not for whom the phone rings; it rings for thee.

10. Y / N   Whom stole the cookies from the jar?

11. Y / N   Aunt Ruth's elephant, Binky, is little.

12. Y / N   I wanted to be a writer; now I are one.

13. Y / N   This test comprises many interesting questions.

14. Y / N   Ain't that the greatest thing you have ever heard?

15. Y / N   Aren't I Aunt Ruth's favorite nauseating nephew?

Lesson 9

Can and May

Are these sentences correct (under normal circumstances)?

Example: Can I play violin tonight after dinner? This would not be correct, unless you somehow might have the ability to play after dinner even though you couldn't before dinner.

1. Y / N   Can I sit in that chair?

2. Y / N   May I go out to dinner with Hank?

3. Y / N   I can throw a baseball.

4. Y / N   I may throw a baseball outside, but not in the house.

5. Y / N   Mr. Musial, can you hit it over the fence?

6. Y / N   Can I walk your dog?

7. Y / N   May I have a piece of that pie?

8. Y / N   Can I have a salad?

9. Y / N   Can I go to college next year?

Use may or can to complete the following sentences.

10. No, you _____ not go to the movie tonight.

11. I _____ eat a whole pizza myself.

12. _____ I have the tape measure, please?

13. _____ I go fishing after breakfast?

Lesson 10

Further and Farther

Are these sentences correct?

1. Y / N I need to look into this issue farther.

2. Y / N I can throw the ball further than you.

3. Y / N I am further along with this book.

4. Y / N For a farthing, my father threw Aunt Ruth's elephant farther.

As and Like

Are the following sentences correct?

1. Y / N   You look as though you saw a lima bean.

2. Y / N   You look like a garbanzo bean.

3. Y / N   You look as though you ate a toad.

4. Y / N   You look like you ate a frog.

5. Y / N   I feel like a koala.

6. Y / N   I feel like I have run the gauntlet.

7. Y / N   Sometimes I feel like a big owl.

8. Y / N   You look as though you don't give a hoot.

9. Y / N   Aunt Ruth waddles like a duck.

10. Y / N He looked as if he were contemplating something deep.

Lesson 11

Review 2

Use who or whom to complete the following sentences.

1. You want to give the broccoli to _____ ?

2. You are going to sing to _____ ?

3. To _____ are you going to sing ?

4. _____ will be the next king?

5. The next king will be _____ ?

6. _____ is going to give what to _____ ?

Are these sentences correct?

7. Y / N   I felt like a million bucks. That's a lot of venison.

8. Y / N   I felt as if I could eat a horse.

9. Y / N   I felt like I could eat a horse.

10. Y / N   He eats cereal like a cat that slurps milk from a bowl.

11. Y / N   You look like Albert Einstein on a bad hair day.

12. Y / N   It looks like it might rain today.

13. Y / N   It was he who answered the telephone.

14. Y / N   I really think I can do this.

Lesson 12

Review 3

Are these sentences correct?

1. Y / N   She gave cookies to Aunt Ruth and me.

2. Y / N   She gave cookies to us.

3. Y / N   He sold his baseball cards to Loretta and I.

4. Y / N   Aunt Ruth and me gave cookies to her.

5. Y / N   Us gave cookies to her.

6. Y / N   Those who have blue umbrellas are we.

7. Y / N   They hoped the blue umbrellas were sent to us.

8. Y / N   I gave the apple pie to she.

9. Y / N   Can I fit into your shoes?

10. Y / N   Can I wear your shoes?

11. Y / N   May I eat your salad?

12. Y / N   Hopefully, I submitted the manuscript to the publisher.

Use lie or lay (or forms thereof) to complete the following sentences.

13. I _____ my coat on the table this morning.

14. I need to _____ my book on the counter for a moment.

15. Yesterday, he _____ down to catch up on rest.

Lesson 13

That and Which

Fill in the blank with the correct word, that or which.

1. The spider _____ sat down beside her was friendly and jovial.

2. The tuba, _____ is my favorite instrument, can lull a hound dog to sleep and send a cat into hysterics at the same time.

3. This is the day _____ the Lord has made. Let us rejoice and be glad!

4. The persimmon _____ is on the counter is yours.

5. The persimmon, _____ is a most unusual fruit, is gaining popularity.

6. The thing _____ has twenty-two legs is crawling up your back.

7. People worry about too many things, but there are few things _____ really matter.

8. Her favorite song, _____ is also one of my favorites, is by Beethoven.

9. _____ board game do you think is the best?

10. Was this the face _____ launched a thousand ships and burnt the topless towers of Ilium?

11. _____ was one of the happiest moments of my life!

12. I am really enjoying the book _____ you gave me.

13. What is the favorite thing _____ you did last summer?

14. Would you rather eat a bowl of ice cream or do these worksheets _____ I gave you?

Lesson 14

If I Were

Are these sentences correct?

1. Y / N If I were not the king, I would not have told them to eat cake.

2. Y / N Well, if I were just a bit taller, I wouldn't fit in my skin.

3. Y / N You say that you saw me in a blue sweatshirt? If I was there, I'd have worn my red sweatshirt. (Hint: I was there.)

4. Y / N If I were you, I'd eat the bratwurst and then the sauerkraut, instead of the other way around.

5. Y / N If I were to rob a bank, I certainly wouldn't go about it the way that he did.

6. Y / N If I was just a little bit older, I would certainly feel younger than I am.

7. Y / N If Jeremiah was a kangaroo instead of a bullfrog, do you think he would still be a really good friend of yours?

8. Y / N If I was an astronaut with a spaceship, just think of all the cool places I could go!

9. Y / N If I were the king of my own little country, I would declare every day to be a grammar holiday.

10. Y / N My boss was Mr. Ware. I always said that if my boss was Ware, then that meant I was working under Ware.

Lesson 15

Verbing or Verbizing

Verbing or verbizing is taking a noun and turning it into a verb. Many words used today were formed that way. For example, we used to give or receive gifts. Now we can gift something. We can even re-gift it, if we care.
The following verbs were all created from nouns originally.

Hospitalizing, Utilizing, Onboarding, Computerizing, Landscaping

Can you come up with some on your own (even silly sounding words are fine, such as tuba-ize)?

_____   _____   _____

_____   _____   _____

Circle all the non-words you find below.

Henry was cooking breakfast when his roommate walked in.
"Hi Henry," said George. "What are you doing?"
"I am omeletting some eggs."
"Mmm. Would you mind omeletting one for me too?"
"No problem. Are you going to do some magazining this morning?"
"No, I magazined last night. I think I'll piano-ize for a while."
"So are you going to Chopinize or Beethovenize today?"
"I think I'll do some Gershwining, actually."
"Oh, your Gershwining is so good ... are you thinking of Rhapsody in Blueing?"
"I thought I might Prelude-ize."
"Hey, I'm going to go orchardize some apples later this morning. They're ripe now."
"Well, if you orchardize, I'll be happy to pie-ize this afternoon."
"Oh man, ice creamizing a hot apple pie would be perfect."
"Oh I love dessertizing!"
"What are you going to breakfastize tomorrow?"
"I'm waffling."

Lesson 16

Anybody and Everybody

Are the following sentences correct?

1. Y / N   Everybody has to do his homework before tomorrow.

2. Y / N   Anybody who wants to can stand up from their seat.

3. Y / N   None of us have ever gone to Mars, except for Aunt Ruth.

4. Y / N   If someone wants to, they can go get food for the rest of us.

5. Y / N   All of them are crazy!

6. Y / N   Every writer has his or her sources of inspiration.

7. Y / N   Everyone thinks they should be first in line.

8. Y / N   Nobody says he thinks that Binky should be president.

9. Y / N   None of them are going to the zoo to see Aunt Ruth.

10. Y / N   Nobody should skip their breakfast!

11. Y / N   Nobody should skip his or her breakfast.

12. Y / N   If anyone thinks Binky is tiny, they're crazy.

13. Y / N   Everybody who has met Aunt Ruth will never forget her.

14. Y / N   Everyone is going to have to tie his shoes before leaving the room.

15. Y / N   Each of the students has to do his or her own homework.

16. Y / N   No one has to do their taxes this year.

17. Y / N   Nobody knows their pets better than Noah.

Lesson 17

Will and Shall

Circle will or shall as appropriate. In cases where either will work, circle both.

1. It's hard to believe that you will / shall be 17 tomorrow!

2. I will / shall go to the ballgame tonight.

3. He will / shall be going to the restaurant this weekend.

4. You will / shall pay homage to me, the king.

5. She will / shall be working this Saturday.

6. She will / shall lead this team, or else I will fire her.

7. I will / shall be there for breakfast in the morning.

8. You will / shall be there too, right?

9. Will / shall he be there also?

10. I will / shall make it through the mountains, or else!

11. We will / shall be going to the play together!

12. Barney was thirsty, so he drew water from the well / shall.

13. Will / Shall Rogers said he never met a man he didn't like.

14. When I die, my will / shall specifies that each of my children will receive a copy of *I Laid an Egg on Aunt Ruth's Head* (autographed, of course).

15. You will / shall pay the rent, or I will evict you!

16. I am determined that I shall / will not pay the rent until you take the elephant away.

Lesson 18

It's and Its

Are these sentences correct?

1. Y / N   Its about time you invited Aunt Ruth over to your house, don't you think?

2. Y / N   Many thought Gerald wanted to escape, but for a content goldfish, escaping was the furthest thing from it's mind.

3. Y / N   I saw a red fox this morning. Its tail was so pretty.

4. Y / N   We have had the family car for ten years now, and I think it's on its last legs.

Fill in the blank with the correct word, either its or it's.

5. It looks like _____ going to be a long day at the park with Aunt Ruth.

6. I found our chicken busily laying _____ eggs on Aunt Ruth's head.

7. Have you ever seen Saturn through a telescope? _____ rings are simply beautiful.

8. _____ time for lunch! I wonder what Aunt Ruth will stir up in her cauldron.

9. How much is the elephant in the window? Yes, I mean the one with _____ ears cut short and _____ tail cut long.

Are these sentences correct?

10. Y / N   It's simply amazing!
11. Y / N   Its another day at the office.
12. Y / N   Its back is scaly and its scalp is furry.
13. Y / N   It's time for Aunt Ruth's birthday celebration.
14. Y / N   It's its tenth time that it's taken food from our bird feeder today!

Lesson 19

Review 4

Select the appropriate words.

1. He laid / lay / lied in bed all last week with the flu.

2. She had laid / lay / lain in bed all last week with pneumonia.

3. I hope that / Hopefully she hung the laundry outside to dry.

4. I hope that / Hopefully the wolf will not get the three little pigs this time.

5. She gave an elephant to Clovis and I / me.

6. To who / whom are you going to sing?

7. May / Can we throw a baseball around after dinner?

8. The committee needs to look at the bill a little further / farther.

9. If I was / were Charlie Chaplin, I would have spoken up better in those movies.

10. Everybody has / have at least two chickens.

11. None of us need / needs to eat dessert at the restaurant tonight.

12. Is it true that you will / shall be playing the tuba next week?

13. Its / It's going to be a long afternoon for the penguin and its / it's pet iguana.

14. Can / May I be excused from this worksheet so I can get back to my writing?

15. I lay / laid the book aside somewhere and now I cannot find it.

16. I was lying / laying down on the couch when Aunt Ruth threw the javelin through the window.

Lesson 20

Parentheses

Correct the punctuation in all sentences found below, keeping all parentheses. If the sentence is already correct, write Correct.

1. Some people can be delightful (like Aunt Ruth.).

2. Some people can be obstreperously stubborn (like Aunt Ruth.)

3. (A standalone sentence such as this can have the punctuation inside the parentheses.)

4. A sentence such as this needs to have the punctuation outside the parentheses (such as this).

5. Remember, you need to be able to remove the entire parenthetical expression without damaging the rest of the sentence, (and this sentence would break).

6. These worksheets are the greatest thing ever (next to traveling to sixteenth century Italy with Aunt Ruth, that is).

7. When I see parentheses, I feel the need to (quietly) whisper (like this.).

8. Some sentences have too many parentheses (but don't you just love these things?).

Lesson 21

Lose and Loose

It seems that when most people get this wrong, it is because they use "loose" when they should use "lose."

Use lose or loose as appropriate.

1. I hope I don't _____ my mind before the day is done.

2. I'm thin now and my pants are too _____.

3. I hope Aunt Ruth doesn't _____ her elephant Binky.

4. Aunt Ruth rarely wears clothes that are too _____.

5. It's possible to play hard and still _____ the ballgame.

6. Attention! The iguana is on the _____.

7. I _____ my car keys frequently.

8. My shoestrings are usually too _____.

9. Do you get mad when you _____ a friendly game?

10. Don't let the dog _____ from his leash or you might _____ him.

11. We are ahead with only two minutes left. I hope we don't _____.

12. Stay calm. Don't _____ your composure.

13. Keep your autographed picture of Aunt Ruth. You don't want to _____ that.

14. Hey, who let Aunt Ruth _____ from her cage?

Lesson 22

Well and Good

Name three things that make you feel good (e.g., reading a book on a rainy day):

1. _____

2. _____

3. _____

Name three things that you want to do well (e.g., play the tuba):

1. _____

2. _____

3. _____

Circle the best answers.

a. You are helping an old lady across the street. You are doing good / doing well.

b. You wake up feeling cheerful, happy, and smiling. Someone asks you how you are. You say: I am well / I am good.

c. Someone asks you how you are doing. You say: I am well / I am good.

d. You have been sick all week, and finally you start to feel better. Someone asks how you feel. You say: I feel well / I feel good.

e. Your hands have poor circulation and the cold weather has made your fingers numb. How do you feel? Not well / Not good.

f. You see a Santa Claus at the mall. He asks you if you have been good or bad. You say: I have been good / I have been well.

Lesson 23

Apostrophes

Circle the 29 apostrophe errors in the story below.

Aunt Ruth once had a pet iguana named Elmer. Now, Elmer had been her's for several year's, and during that time Elmer had developed some odd habit's.

It's first interesting habit occurred each day when it would go out and get the two morning newspaper's. That wasnt the odd part. The odd part was that Elmer would sing the newspapers contents loudly on the street corner, accompanied by his little electric guitar. Its singing wasnt bad for an iguana, and it's guitar playing was pretty good. Elmer's rendition of Iguana Hold Your Hand made the Top 40 Reptile Hit's, second only to a version of Godzilla as performed by the Purple Mussel Followers'.

Its second quirk was that it would only take it's bath's each night at midnight, and it's preferred water temperature was ice cold. Aunt Ruth would diligently scrub it's back and under its arms, and then she would brush its teeth. Elmer was also good about having it's teeth flossed.

Elmers skin had bright color's, especially in the sunshine. The blue's, silver's, green's, and sometimes even the red's would show off nicely. Elmers photographs appealed to many advertising agent's, and Elmer received offers from some of Madison Avenues biggest name's.

The iguana loved New York City, but he missed Aunt Ruth and her wacky adventures. Occasionally, Aunt Ruth's mailbox would contain a letter from Elmer, and this always delighted her. Then, on one fine spring afternoon, Aunt Ruth opened her mailbox and was surprised to see Elmer standing inside, smiling at her.

They hugged and danced, and then they went out and ate a couple of pizza's.

Elmer went to nearby Iguana University and became a writer of grammar book's. Elmer kept in touch with Aunt Ruth—in fact, for years they had breakfast together on Saturday's—and Elmers life was filled with happiness for ever after.

Lesson 24

Real and Really

Are these sentences correct?

1. Y / N   I saw a real good movie.

2. Y / N   He's a really interesting person.

3. Y / N   The loss was a real blow for morale.

4. Y / N   Yes, I really am going to invite Aunt Ruth over for dinner.

5. Y / N   When I go fishing, I like to use a rod and real.

6. Y / N   It was a real dark and stormy night.

7. Y / N   That's a really great book.

Find the four errors in the story below.

Bobbi had a real good time at the state fair. First, she bought some cotton candy, made from real maple syrup. It was really cheap, so she bought a lot of it (and ate it all). Then she bought some peanuts, and they were really good.

While walking through the Midway, Bobbi saw something really shocking – life-sized chocolate elephants. She was not really hungry, so she only bought one chocolate elephant. It weighed 300 pounds—really heavy! Bobbi sat down and ate the real big chocolate elephant fairly quickly, finishing in about 15 minutes. When she finished, she felt so full, and she began to worry. She was real concerned because she had eaten so much that she thought she would explode.

At that moment, someone accidentally dropped a candied apple from the ferris wheel, and it landed on top of Bobbi's head. The people in the crowd held their breaths a long time; they were really worried that Bobbi would pop. She didn't though, and the crowd was real happy.

Bobbi never really ate that much bad food again, ever. That's the real truth.

Lesson 25

There, They're, and Their

Find the fourteen incorrect uses of there, their, or they're in the story below.

Their once was a dog who had a pet boy, and they liked to spend they're time out in the woods. On one of there outings, the boy saw two cats. He said, "Look Fido, those cats are fishing, but their using there fishing poles instead of they're claws. They don't have any bait on they're hooks"

Fido looked at the cats and they're fishing poles.

The cats looked at Fido and the boy and noticed that they were staring at their fishing poles. They didn't like people staring at their fishing poles, but they decided it would be in their best interest if they continued their fishing.

Then the boy said, "Should we go help them with there fishing?"

Fido smiled and wiggled his ears.

The boy said, "Okay, come with me. We'll show them how to put bait on the hooks. They'll need to know that if their going to catch any fish."

Fido smiled at the boy and said, "You're right! I think they're going to need to learn how to fish."

The boy looked at Fido and said, "Hey wait, you can talk!"

Fido looked at the boy and said, "Their, their, don't be too surprised. We're just characters in a story, remember?"

After the dog and his pet boy helped teach the cats how to fish, they walked back to they're house, where they spent the rest of there days living happily ever after.

Lesson 26

Your, You're, and Yours

Are these sentences correct?

1. Y / N   Your the apple of my eye.

2. Y / N   I think this is you're dog.

3. Y / N   What is your cat doing here?

4. Y / N   You're so funny!

5. Y / N   This is yours, not mine.

6. Y / N   How did you spend you're evening?

7. Y / N   Your not serious, are you?

8. Y / N   Your not sure where your going until you get in you're car and drive a while.

9. Y / N   I believe this is you're possum sandwich.

10. Y / N   Aunt Ruth? No, she's not my aunt. She's your's.

11. Y / N   I hope your kidding!

12. Y / N   I thought you said you're dog didn't bite.

13. Y / N   This is you're book, is it not?

14. Y / N   You're acting a bit goofy this morning.

15. Y / N   Why, I do believe that these are yours.

16. Y / N   Wait, your kidding, right?

Lesson 27

Myriad, Complimentary, and Stationery

Find all four incorrect words in the story below.

The boy and his father were out walking in the fields in the middle of October. Even though it was the middle of the day, the sky suddenly became dark. "Look," the boy exclaimed, "the cattle are all migrating south for the winter."

Sure enough, the father looked up only to see myriad cattle flying south. The father complemented his son, saying, "Son, you sure have good eyes."

The boy remained stationery while the father pulled out his best stationary and wrote a letter home, telling his wife about this event. It wasn't all that common to see a myriad of cattle flying south in broad daylight (usually they do their flying at night). In fact, some people still believed that the story of the cow jumping over the moon was only a myth.

One of the cows, a chocolate Guernsey, spotted the boy and his father below, and he diverted his path and landed right in front of them. He bowed low, greeted them with a friendly "moo," and held out a gallon jug of ice cold chocolate milk.

"Thank you," said the father, "but we haven't any money with us. We have no way of paying for chocolate milk."

"Oh, no problem," said the cow. "This is complementary."

"Well thanks," said the father. With that, the cow curtsied and took off to catch up with the myriad cattle flying south for the winter.

At that moment, the jug of chocolate milk spoke. "Say there, I like those boots you're wearing, boy. And Mister, that's a mighty fine hat you are wearing, if I do say so myself."

"Thank you," said the polite son. He turned to his father and said, "Dad, the cow was right. This milk really is complimentary!"

Lesson 28

Irregardless and Other Non-Words

Find the twenty non-words (including repeats) in the story below.

Ms. Wigglethorpe was standing in the aisle at the local grocer, trying to decide whether to get the flammable or inflammable hair spray. She was in a quandary, struggling with the decision. Irregardless of what she would decide, she felt it was a lose-lose situation. If she opted for the flammable, it might go up in flames. If she opted for the inflammable, it too might end up in flames. Either way could be not fun.

From the back corner of the store, a man emerged wearing a black suit made from lamb's wool. It was a new fashion they call a baaxedo. The man spoke.

"Enpicture if you will a certain Mrs Wigglethorpe, who was conflubbulated while trying to make an inshopillent decision. Little did she realize that she had become superenzoned ... in the Hair Spray Enigma."

Much to her annoyment, when she orientated herself back toward the front window of the store, she noticed that there was quite a big storm coming. She did some quick analyzation and decided that the inclimate weather would be okay, even though her hair might get wet.

Mrs. Wigglethorpe stared at the man—she was quite the staremeister—but then she broke into a fit of laughication when she realized he was wearing a baaxedo.

"Why, you are wearing a baaxedo!" she exclaimed. "You may not have awareized it, but I am the designer of the baaxedo. It is the centerpiece of my magnificent new line of clothing, baaxiwear."

"You invented baaxiwear?" the man asked inquiriously.

"Yesdeed," she smiled, with great cheek liftication. "Soon, you will even be able to purchase our new line of male undergarments."

"Oh?" he asked, in a most querisitive manner. "What will they be called?"

"Baaxer shorts," she said with a jovialacious laugh.

Lesson 29

Review 5

Select the appropriate words.

1. I'm not sure how this happens, but Aunt Ruth seems to consistently loose / lose her pet elephant Binky.

2. The night was real / really awful. Binky fell on me while attempting a cartwheel.

3. So, my head hurt and I just wasn't feeling very well / good when I woke up this morning.

4. "Say, that's a nice tie your / you're wearing," said Binky, who was more complementary / complimentary than the average elephant.

5. Where do elephants keep luggage? In they're / there / their trunks, of course.

6. Binky did not move all day. He was quite stationary / stationery.

7. With a pencil, the little girl wrote a letter on Binky's side. She must have thought Binky was stationary / stationery.

8. Their / They're going to the zoo tomorrow, where they hope to see myriad of / myriad animals.

9. Your / You're certain that those are your / you're plans for the afternoon?

10. Regardless / Irregardless, I hope you show up at the restaurant.

Rewrite the following sentences to use punctuation for parentheses correctly.

11. Binky loves jazz music (his favorite artist is Elephant Gerald.)

12. Binky can use his trunk to play notes higher than any jazz trumpeter, (except for Maynard Ferguson).

Lesson 30

Capitalization

Find the thirteen capitalization errors.

1. Raleigh is the capital of North Carolina and should be capitalized. I think that richmond, as the capital of Virginia, should be capitalized too.

2. I went to see Professor Aunt Ruth about the test she had given us yesterday. The Professor was in a jolly mood and she said that she would give me an A. I said this to her: "I have a question for you, professor. Should I capitalize the word professor or not?"

3. She said, "It depends."

4. I had a dream that I met the mayor, the governor, and the president. None of them looked capitalized in the dream. Should they be capitalized in real life? The mayor, Mayor Smith, should have the first word capitalized when it's used with the name or when he/she is being directly addressed. The mayor is funny. You, Mayor, are funny.

5. Of course, names such as Max, George, and benjamin need to be capitalized. Titles such as Dr., Mrs., and mr. should be capitalized too.

6. People tend to capitalize words that seem important, but they shouldn't be capitalized. The chief Topic for today is Capitalization.

7. The Grand Canyon is beautiful, or so I have heard. I have not seen it. I hope to See it someday!

8. I wonder if the president wants to take this test? Hello, President, would you like to do these worksheets?

9. I think this is a Capital Idea!

10. Many states in the United States have changed their Capitals over the years.

11. One does not receive Capital Punishment for missing capital letters.

Lesson 31

Split Infinitives

Find the split infinitives (there should be thirteen).

The town came to a standstill as the stranger rode into town on horseback. A chill swept the air; a tumbleweed blew down the street, getting caught on a wagon wheel in front of the barber shop; and a tuba was heard, playing a Bach fugue softly in the background.

The stranger adjusted his cowboy hat and walked into the saloon.

1. "I would like a banana split infinitive please."

2. "Would you like that to enjoyably eat here or to quickly go?"

3. "Oh, you like to really confuse me, don't you!"

4. "I tend to quite enjoy that, yes."

5. "Well then, I'd like to really have my banana split infinitive here."

6. "Are you going to additionally order anything else?"

7. "You mean like whipped cream, a maraschino cherry, and perhaps some chocolate syrup to ravenously devour?"

8. "I had wanted to sarcastically ask you if you wanted a diet soda with that, but I should decline the temptation to rudely bother you with that question."

9. "That's so kind of you. You are a gentleman seeking to pleasantly help the customers around you to thoroughly enjoy their desserts."

10. "Say, you're not from around here, are you?"

11. "Well no, but I've got to thankfully tip my hat to you ... these banana split infinitives are so good I want to quickly inhale another one!"

Lesson 32

Dangling Participles

Fix the dangling participles and misplaced modifiers below.

Example: Flying high overhead, Vic saw the ducks from his hidden duck blind.

(Fixed): From behind his duck blind, Vic saw the ducks flying high overhead.

1. Raining heavily—in fact, it was an absolutely torrential downpour—I made it from my car to the house without getting too wet.

2. Spicier than I normally like, I ate the whole plate of Mexican food that was placed in front of me.

3. Barking all night long, I was kept awake by the dogs across the street.

4. Spiraling through the air, I made the perfect pass for the winning touchdown in the football game.

5. Cheesy and bubbling and piping hot, I love eating macaroni and cheese on a cold autumn day.

Lesson 33

Whoever and Whomever

Select whoever or whomever.

1. You can be whoever / whomever you want to be when you grow up.

2. I will give the chocolate covered raisins to whoever / whomever wants them.

3. This ticket is for whoever / whomever wants to go to the game.

4. The football flew through the air and decided to land on whoever / whomever it pleased.

5. The phone is ringing for whoever / whomever wants to answer it.

6. The roses on the table are for whoever / whomever.

7. Aunt Ruth is saving the fruitcake for whoever / whomever she wants to have it—she made it seventeen years ago.

8. The bell will toll for whoever / whomever it wants to toll.

9. Whoever / Whomever wants to eat now, the food is ready!

10. Whoever / Whomever said it is a small world?

11. To whoever / whomever it may concern ...

12. Someone took my tooth brush by accident! I hope that whoever / whomever has it will not be crestfallen.

13. To whoever / whomever it was who borrowed my aardvark, I do wish you would return it.

14. To whoever / whomever she gave the fruitcake, she also gave an indelible and inedible memory.

Lesson 34

Using Past Participles

Select the correct word.

Aunt Ruth decided, one fine summer day, to go for a swim.

1. A goose who swam / swum every day in the pond was already there.

2. Aunt Ruth saw the goose and swam / swum toward it.

3. The goose swam / swum across the pond, trying to get away from Aunt Ruth.

4. Aunt Ruth has swam / swum after this particular goose before, trying to have it over for dinner.

5. If Aunt Ruth had swam / swum faster, she may have caught the goose.

6. The dinner bell had rang / rung, and the goose thought this was a warning signal to be on the lookout for Aunt Ruth.

7. The dinner bell rang / rung yesterday, too.

8. Aunt Ruth was not intending to eat the goose; if Aunt Ruth had brung / brought an invitation before, the goose would have realized that Aunt Ruth wanted to have it over for dinner as a guest, not as the main course.

9. Aunt Ruth brang / brought an invitation this time, but the goose refused to get close enough to read it.

10. After the goose swam across the lake, he ran / run. After he had ran / run a ways, he finally was too tired to run further. Aunt Ruth caught him and invited him for dinner. He was delighted.

What a silly language. What a silly goose!

Lesson 35

Many and Much

Where given a choice, select the correct word.

Once upon a time there was a boy who had too much / many aunts. He had an Aunt Spoony, an Aunt Rubella, an Aunt Edsel, an Aunt Emeraldine, an Aunt Euphoria, an Aunt Dropsy, an Aunt Bugsy, an Aunt Doodle, an Aunt Sycamore, and an Aunt Ruth. They all lived with the boy in a house without much / many space.

Believe it or not, on his birthday he complained because he received too much / many birthday presents from his aunts. They gave him too much / many building blocks, too much / many writing paper, too much / many birthday cake with too much / many candles, too much / many books, and too much / many milk. He simply did not have room for all of it—he had too much / many stuff!

Then it came to pass that the boy grew older—in fact, he grew much / many older, and after much / many years he ended up older than the aunts. How did that happen? I don't know. But the fact is that he was older than his aunts, and this gave him much / many delight.

Now, when it was his much / many aunts' birthdays, he would give them some of the much / many things that they had given him over the years.

For a while, there was much / many complaining by the aunts. After all, they didn't have much / many space to put their stuff either. They had too much / many things! It was just too much / many stuff.

For much / many days, the much / many aunts sat on the front porch in their much / many rocking chairs, pondering what to do. They all agreed with much / many enthusiasm that something needed to be done, but they couldn't figure out what to do. There were so much / many options. It was much / many too confusing.

Then, Aunt Ruth had a great idea. "Let's sell much / many of this stuff, getting rid of much / many things. We can then give the money to people who need it more than we do."

There was much / many rejoicing at this idea, and they all lived much / many happy years together in that house.

Lesson 36

Between, Among, Next, This

Select the correct word.

1. Between / Among the five of us, we should be able to select who's going to take Aunt Ruth to the movies.

2. Between / Among the two of us, we should be able to select who's going to take Aunt Ruth shopping.

3. Between / Among you and me, we should be able to select who's going to go skydiving with Aunt Ruth.

4. Aunt Ruth and her parachute landed between / among the trees in the forest.

5. On her next jump, Aunt Ruth landed between / among your house, Elmer's house, and my house.

6. Between / Among the six of us, we were able to collect enough money to buy Aunt Ruth a diet soda.

7. Let's meet at the restaurant between / among 7:30 and 7:45 tomorrow night.

8. Choose a number between / among one and ten.

9. If today is Tuesday, then this / next Wednesday is a week from tomorrow.

10. If today is Tuesday, then this / next Wednesday is tomorrow.

11. This / Next Thursday is the matinée. Today is Monday. The matinée is three days away.

Lesson 37

Principle, Principal, Accept, Except

Select the correct word.

1. The book *I Laid an Egg on Aunt Ruth's Head* is based on some of the fundamental principals / principles of grammar.

2. I think that the principal / principle of each school should make the book required reading for all the students.

3. When will people accept / except the responsibility to speak correctly?

4. Everyone took his animal to the pet show, accept / except for Aunt Ruth. She had a tough time getting Binky in the car.

5. I just cannot accept / except the fact that Binky won't play with me.

6. Accept / Except for Thursday night, I'm busy every night this week.

7. I went to the bank to pay off the principal / principle amount of the loan.

8. They would not accept / except my cash. They said they would only accept / except books about Aunt Ruth instead.

9. I was at the ceremony to accept / except the award for Aunt Ruth, who somehow had found herself glued to the ceiling of her apartment and was unable to come.

10. The martian invasion was the scariest thing I had ever experienced, accept / except for the first time I met Aunt Ruth.

11. This organization has certain principles / principals, or guidelines, that we must follow if we are to be successful.

Lesson 38

Review 6

Select the appropriate words.

1. I think whomever / whoever wants it can have it.

2. Take this grilled cheese sandwich and give it to whomever / whoever.

3. I have swam / swum in that pond.

4. The bell had rang / rung last month.

5. There is not much / many sand, but there are many / much grains of sand.

6. Between / Among the two of us, I think that soda is overrated.

7. Can you accept / except that the principals / principles of grammar are important to Aunt Ruth?

Find the capitalization errors in this paragraph.

    the day i went to see The President, He was golfing on the Front Lawn. He asked me how I was. I told him I was fine, and then I said, "Mr. President, do you want to have lunch with me?" He thought that was a Grand Idea, so we went to Aunt ruth's new restaurant. Binky was the Chef.

Find the split infinitives in this paragraph.

    To courageously fight for what one believes in is important; to bravely stand up for one's ideals, however, is not to brashly say that we shouldn't be tolerant of others. They have the right to likewise defend their beliefs.

Rewrite the sentence below to fix the dangling participle.

    Rising high into the deep blue sky, I noticed the sun on this beautiful day.

Lesson 39

Wake, Awake, e.g., i.e.

Select the correct word.

1. Aunt Ruth needs to wake / awake up or she will miss the waffles that Binky is making for breakfast.

2. Aunt Ruth was awakened / wokened when there was a raven knocking on her door.

3. Aunt Ruth woke / waked up when Bill the Grammar Fairy came and played the tuba in her room.

4. She awoke / awokened when the bulldozer accidentally knocked down her bedroom wall.

5. After she woke up, Aunt Ruth prepared some of her favorite food, e.g. / E.I.E.I.O., buttermilk pancakes.

6. My favorite color, i.e. / e.g., blue, is in the United States flag.

7. I plan to study Industrial Engineering as my major when I go to college, i.e. / e.g., I.E.

8. I tend to enjoy listening to brass instruments (e.g. / i.e., tuba) more than woodwinds or strings.

9. Aunt Ruth was wakened / wokened by the sounds of a tuba quartet serenading her on her front lawn.

10. I awoke / awoked when Aunt Ruth knocked on my door at 2 a.m.

11. Some pieces of literature, i.e. / e.g., *I Laid an Egg on Aunt Ruth's Head*, are simply magnificent works of art.

Lesson 40

Dessert, Desert

Select the correct word.

1. My favorite deserts / desserts all have chocolate in them.

2. I figuratively / literally felt as though I were about a zillion years old this morning when I woke up.

3. Can you ensure / insure that Aunt Ruth never gives me another fruit cake?

4. The Sahara desert / dessert is one of the most impressive in all the world.

5. I figuratively / literally forgot where I was supposed to be last night.

6. You should ensure / insure your tuba against possible theft or damage.

7. May we have some desert / dessert after dinner tonight?

8. He figuratively / literally can throw the ball a million miles an hour.

9. Well son, I want you to ensure / insure that it never happens again.

10. I've figuratively / literally told you a billion times that you need to clean your plate off if you expect to get any desert / dessert.

11. I'm so glad my car was ensured / insured! Who would have expected someone to drop one of Aunt Ruth's fruitcakes from a bridge onto my car?

12. Waiter, there's a camel in my desert / dessert.

13. Surrounded by billions upon billions of grains of sand, Lawrence saw it. There, on top of a mound of sand, was a maraschino cherry. "Somebody," he thought to himself, "has made a big mistake. This place is a desert / dessert."

Lesson 41

Alright and All Right

Select the correct word.

1. Alright / All right folks, it's time to get this show on the road.

2. Hey dude, I hope you are feeling alright / all right.

3. I like this book a lot / alot.

4. A lot / Alot of people are coming to see Aunt Ruth go bungee jumping.

Rewrite each sentence so that it is correct.

5. This fruitcake from 1969 needs eaten.

6. Your cat needs washed.

7. Your teeth need brushed.

Lesson 42

Apostrophes in Names

Find the seventeen errors.

Rubys' dog was a very strange animal. Its name was Rover, but that's not why it was strange. It was strange because it could speak English.

Rovers favorite thing to do on a sunny Saturday afternoon was to go to the park and swing on the swing set. There, Rover would see the Jones family with their 17 kid's, and he would see the Smith's with their one kid. The Smiths' had cousins' who would come to visit sometime's, and they would always bring present's.

Once the Smiths cousin's brought liver pudding, and another time they brought souse. If you have never had souse, you're in for a real treat. Its a food thats popular in some part's of the United State's.

(Its very hard to inject errors' on purpose. You should try this sometime's.)

Select the correct word.

1. My advise / advice to you is to get out of Dodge as fast as you can. Aunt Ruth is comin', and she means business.

2. I think that's good advise / advice, son. I'll bolt the doors on the saloon and we'll see if Aunt Ruth can get past that.

3. I had a boss once who gave me this advise / advice: If you want to dance, you've got to pay the fiddler.

4. Do you need someone to advice / advise you on how to do this worksheet?

Lesson 43

Review 7

Select the appropriate words.

1. I hope Aunt Ruth wakes / awakes up in time to take Binky out for a walk.

2. My favorite dessert / desert is the Sahara, though I get thirsty just thinking about it.

3. I was literally / figuratively starving to death last night during the show.

4. All right / Alright folks, we've got to leave if we're going to see Binky star in Aunt Ruth's latest movie.

5. I like chocolate a lot / alot.

6. The only advise / advice I can give you is that two elephants in one little apartment might not be a good idea.

7. That's just a dessert / desert that needs to be / needs eaten.

8. Old MacDonald had a farm with many different kinds of animals, i.e., / e.g., a big cow.

9. Mrs. MacDonald loved living on the farm and reaping the many benefits of country living, e.g. / i.e., fresh eggs every morning.

Find the errors in apostrophes in the paragraph below.

    Once upon a time, there was an elderly woman named Effie. Now, Effies favorite food to eat was macaraoni's and cheese. She also liked trying graham crackers' in a bowl of milk at time's. Effies aunt was Aunt Ruth, and Aunt Ruths favorite thing to do was to take Effie shopping, especially to the hat store. One day they were passing by the fish market, and Aunt Ruth asked Effie if she wanted a salmon. Effie said she loved salmon's, so Aunt Ruth bought her one. Effie put it on her head, and from that day on she never wore any of her other hats'.

Lesson 44

Affect, Effect, and Unique

Select the correct word.

1. Is your sleep affected / effected when I put my tuba to your ear at night?

2. I've heard that reading grammar books can affect / effect your mind in detrimental ways.

3. Do you notice any affect / effect when you try to think about lie and lay while standing on your head?

4. I'm not sure how knowing Aunt Ruth will affect / effect you, but be assured that there will be some long lasting affects / effects from which you will never fully recover.

5. That movie had some very interesting sound affects / effects.

6. What do you suppose the affect / effect would be if we turned up the guitar amplifier all the way?

7. Caffeine affects / effects different people in different ways.

Rewrite the following sentences so they are correct.

8. Sam was thrilled because Aunt Ruth's letter included a very unique postage stamp of a hen on somebody's head.

9. The first time Aunt Ruth thought she was stepping into the time machine, she ended up in the washing machine. The spin cycle effected her for months.

Lesson 45

Comma Usage I

Fix the comma errors in the following sentences. Add or remove commas where needed.

1. "Hey" said Aunt Ruth "get back here and eat your dinner."

2. Kids I need you to eat every carrot tomato and pea on your plate.

3. I went to the post office to pick up a package and then to the grocery store to pick up some stomach relief medicine.

4. I went to the hospital to have the doctor remove the fruitcake I had eaten and then I went to the post office to mail the fruitcake back to Aunt Ruth.

5. Aunt Ruth for my birthday gave me twenty-seven cents two aluminum TV dinner trays an expired ticket to Palm Springs and a purebred Guernsey cow.

6. Always one to worry Aunt Ruth the indomitable one rarely overlooks details especially the seemingly insignificant ones.

7. Written by Carl Sandburg the biography of Lincoln that I am reading, is really good.

Lesson 46

Comma Usage II

Indicate whether the sentences below correctly use commas. Rewrite the sentences that use commas incorrectly.

1. Y / N   At the football game, Aunt Ruth ordered seven hamburgers, five large fries, three onion rings, and a small diet cola.

2. Y / N   At the basketball game, Aunt Ruth ordered five hot dogs, three large nachos and a bowl of ice cream.

3. Y / N   First, I need you, to wash the dishes very carefully.

4. Y / N   Eat every carrot, and pea on your plate.

5. Y / N   Jeremy the spider is on your shoulder (Jeremy is not a spider).

6. Y / N   Aunt Ruth said, "Say, that's not an elephant."

7. Y / N   The elephant said "Say, that's not a great aunt."

8. Y / N   The elephant, said "The other night, I shot an aunt in my pajamas."

9. Y / N   Aunt Ruth, the adventurous one was off on another escapade.

10. Y / N   "I think I need to tell you this," said Aunt Ruth, "and then I'll tell you that."

Lesson 47

Nauseous and Nauseated

Read the following and answer the questions.

Aunt Ruth was nauseous. Which of the following is the best answer?

a.   Aunt Ruth wasn't feeling well.

b.   Aunt Ruth caused me to not feel well.

c.   It is an ambiguous statement and could mean either (a) or (b).

Which statements below are true, as described in the book?

d.   If something is nauseous, it always makes someone nauseated.

e.   If something is nauseous, it may make someone nauseated, or it may be nauseated itself.

Led and Lead

Select the correct word in the sentence below.

1. Yesterday, Aunt Ruth lead / led a whole herd of lemmings over a cliff.

2. Be careful—Aunt Ruth is carrying around an umbrella made out of lead / led.

3. He has successfully lead / led armies in the past. I think we can leave him in charge of Little Big Horn.

4. It is not the case that you have to be a world leader in order to contract led / lead poisoning.

5. I'm not sure how to get there—you had better lead / led the way.

Lesson 48

Phenomena, Criteria, and Data

In the sentences below, select the best choice for each question.

1. The single criterion / criteria for choosing the candidate is based solely on his or her command of English grammar.

2. There are many criterion / criteria we should use when evaluating this decision.

3. The history of weather has included some strange phenomena / phenomenon over the years.

4. The triple play is a most unusual phenomenon / phenomena in baseball.

5. One piece of data / datum suggests that we should be eating grammar crackers for breakfast.

Historic, Historical, Whether, and If

In the sentences below, select the best choice for each question.

1. The landing of the Pilgrims at Plymouth Rock in 1620 was a historic / historical event that will never be forgotten.

2. We have historic / historical records of my grandparents and great grandparents, some of the early settlers in Nebraska.

3. You should call the radio station to determine whether / if it might rain this afternoon.

4. Let me know whether / if you decide to go to the game (I only want to know if your decision is affirmative).

5. Let me know either way if / whether you decide to go to the game.

Lesson 49

Review 8

Select the appropriate words.

1. How does being related to Aunt Ruth affect / effect your daily life?

2. Most people think that Aunt Ruth is a unique / very unique character.

3. Did you notice any unusual affects / effects after dining with Aunt Ruth?

4. Those fumes are nauseous / nauseated—they make me feel sick.

5. Jake lead / led the expedition up the mountain .

6. Every year there are several phenomena / phenomenon surrounding Aunt Ruth that just cannot be explained.

7. The primary criteria / criterion for being on Aunt Ruth's good side is simply to not lay an egg on her head.

8. With our metal detector, we were able to find an old wagon wheel (I think belonging to Aunt Ruth's first vehicle) and a few other historic / historical artifacts deep in the woods.

9. Try to let me know whether / if you are going to come (I only need to know if you do decide to come).

10. Try to let me know whether / if you are going to come (let me know either way).

Rewrite the following sentences so they are correct.

11. I ran, and played.

12. I ate broccoli a bratwurst, and chocolate.

13. "Larry, don't forget to bring home your laundry", said Mrs. Sauerkraut.

Lesson 50

Comprehensive Review Part 1

Select the appropriate words.

Chapter 1

1. Most people do not realize that Ruth Van Winkle once laid / lay down and slept for twenty years.

2. Just lie / lay the liver on a shelf in the fridge. Aunt Ruth will pick it up tomorrow.

3. I have lied / lain / laid on a water bed.

4. I laid / lay the blanket on the water bed.

Chapter 2

5. Hopefully, / I hope that she won't forget to take Binky on the ferris wheel.

6. Hopefully, / I hope that the farmer planted the seeds in the field.

7. Hopefully, / I hope that I went walking without an umbrella.

8. Hopefully, / I hope that she remembers to meet me at the right location.

Chapter 3

9. You're acting a small / little grumpy this morning.

10. I was a small / little upset when I learned Aunt Ruth had borrowed my jet pack.

11. Aunt Ruth is a little / small country and a little / small rock and roll.

Lesson 51

Comprehensive Review Part 2

Select the appropriate words.

Chapter 4

1. Yes, I am he / him.

2. Yes, this is he / him.

3. She gave the meatloaf to Hank and me / I.

4. Ask not for who / whom the bell tolls, but watch out for that falling piano.

Chapter 5

5. Am / Are I not the king?

6. Aren't / Amn't I the king?

7. You aren't / ain't as crazy as Aunt Ruth said you were.

8. You're looking for Aunt Ruth's nephew? That's me / I.

Chapter 6

One or more sentences below is incorrect. Rewrite the incorrect sentence(s).

9. Twenty-two baseball cards comprise my collection.

10. Seventeen chickens and four kids comprise my family.

11. Aunt Ruth's vocabulary is comprised of many idioms.

12. Aunt Ruth's fruitcake comprises all the necessary ingredients with which to build a small brick wall.

Lesson 52

Comprehensive Review Part 3

Select the appropriate words.

Chapter 7

1. Can / May I have a turn throwing the pie at Aunt Ruth?

2. Can / May you leap a tall building in a single bound?

3. Can / May I have another bratwurst, please?

4. Can / May you play the tuba?

Chapter 8

5. I think Aunt Ruth needs to look into this electric casket warmer idea a little farther / further.

6. I have studied Hamlet a little farther / further in depth than you have.

7. I think I can throw Aunt Ruth a bit farther / further than you can.

8. I think I can throw Aunt Ruth a bit farther / further than I can throw you.

Chapter 9

9. You look as though / like you just saw Aunt Ruth.

10. Aunt Ruth looks as / like Albert Einstein on a bad hair day.

11. I feel like / as a blob of strawberry jello this morning.

12. You look as though / like you want to say something important.

Lesson 53

Comprehensive Review Part 4

Select the appropriate words.

Chapter 10

1. The tuba which / that Aunt Ruth plays is a nice horn.

2. This book, which / that is the author's first, is my favorite of all.

3. The elephant that / which is in the corner—yes, the one sipping a lemonade—is Aunt Ruth's.

4. The rock band which / that Aunt Ruth plays in is too loud for me.

Chapter 11

5. If I was / were smarter, I wouldn't have made that mistake.

6. If I were / was a professional baseball player, I'd jump for joy.

7. If I were / was the king of a small island, I'd eat coconuts every day.

8. If you knew I was / were at the game, why did you ask me if I went?

Chapter 12

Circle the examples of verbing or verbizing that you find.

9. The writer has decided to author a book.

10. It is our turn to host the party.

11. I shall be breakfasting a bit earlier than usual, I'm afraid.

12. Any idea what you're going to be gifting him for his birthday?

Lesson 54

Comprehensive Review Part 5

Select the appropriate words.

Chapter 13

1. Each person needs to brush his / their own teeth.

2. None of us are / is exempt from the laws of grammar.

3. Anybody can go get a drink of water if they want / he wants.

4. Everybody wishes that he or she / they can have an Aunt Ruth.

Chapter 14

5. Do you think you shall / will go to the movies tomorrow night?

6. I think he will / shall laugh when he hears your story.

7. I think I will / shall spend the evening reading a book.

8. It sounds like you will / shall go to the store in the morning, right?

Chapter 15

9. Its / It's a good thing you are doing this lesson right now!

10. The hair on it's / its back was a neon green.

11. It's / its it's / its own master.

12. It's / its a long row to weed.

13. Its / It's most amazing attributes are that it's / its purple, it's / its fuzzy, and it's / its crawling up Aunt Ruth's back.

Lesson 55

Comprehensive Review Part 6

Chapter 16

Keeping the parentheses, rewrite and correct the following sentences.

1. Aunt Ruth (the paragon of rational thinking), put her groceries in an aquarium.

2. Aunt Ruth washed her hair with sauerkraut (her favorite food.)

3. I need to buy chocolate (my favorite comfort food) some bread, and a cow.

Chapter 17

Select the appropriate words.

4. Aunt Ruth is afraid to go jogging because she looses / loses her way even when she is running in place.

5. My shoelaces are too tight. Could you help me make them lose / loose?

6. Even the best team will lose / loose a game.

Chapter 18

Select the appropriate words.

7. I got an A on my test; the flowers are blooming, and Aunt Ruth is coming over for dinner. Life is good / well!

8. My fingertips are numb. I don't feel good / well.

9. How am I doing? I am doing good / well, thank you.

Lesson 56

Comprehensive Review Part 7

Chapter 19

Circle all the errors with apostrophes you find.

I love these apostrophe's. Their tendency to become possessive can be annoying in a way, because apostrophe's can tell us that Jeff's car is a purple van, or Kim's chocolate chip cookie's are hidden on top of the fridge. Theyre also useful for contraction's, letting us say that your babys due in moment's. In general, theyre useful. They help us to know that a dogs' best friend is pizza, or that an elephants trunk isn't something to take lightly but it's great for long trip's. Its really a great thing, wouldn't you agree? If we asked people, I think most would agree we should keep apostrophe's; we just need to be careful how we use them.

Circle the appropriate words in the sentences below.

Chapter 20

1. That movie is really / real good.

2. That bad man is real / really bad.

3. The real real estate lady is really / real pleasant.

4. Real / Really, real men eat quiche.

Chapter 21

5. Their / They're likely to get upset in airport security if you tell them you are from Mars.

6. There / They're is a better way to do this, you know.

7. There / Their pumpkin weighs over four hundred pounds!

8. There / They're is they're / their suitcase that there / they're taking with them.

Lesson 57

Comprehensive Review Part 8

Select the appropriate words.

Chapter 22

1. Your / You're sitting on my possum.

2. Yours / Your's is the one with the purple feathers.

3. You're / Your the first one to speak at Aunt Ruth's coronation ceremony.

4. I do believe the tuba that fell out the window is your's / yours.

Chapter 23

5. That brown tie does not compliment / complement your gray shirt.

6. Please, take another trip in the time machine—it's complementary / complimentary.

7. Hand me that paper please. I am writing a letter and need stationary / stationery.

Chapter 24

8. Regardless / Irregardless, I think you shouldn't have hit her over the head with that fruitcake. I was going to start building a retaining wall in the backyard with it.

9. Irregardless / Regardless of who will be there, to whom will you give the hedgehog?

10. Regardless / Irregardless of the circumstances, the fact is that Aunt Ruth ate three whole cheesecakes in one sitting.

11. Irregardless / Regardless of the fact that Aunt Ruth was dining with the Queen, Aunt Ruth fell asleep in the Queen's comfy chair.

Lesson 58

Comprehensive Review Part 9

Chapter 25

Find the capitalization errors.

the man walked down to the market on a Fine saturday morning, trying to find something to Eat. He was Extremely Hungry and he bought the first thing he saw, which was five pounds of bratwurst from Bratwurst Unlimited. He was happy with his Acquisition and was about to leave, but he saw his friend the Mayor and walked over to talk with him. The man greeted the Mayor—this was mayor Ed, by the way—and the Mayor returned the greeting. The mayor then told the man about a new vendor at the market who was selling birds, and they were Delicious. now, this wasn't just any kind of bird. It was a sea bird. the man was sad because he had spent all his Money, but the Mayor suggested the man selling the birds might be willing to Trade. the man walked over, introduced himself, and he was delighted to find that the vendor indeed would trade. So the man took a Tern for the Wurst.

Chapter 26

Find the split infinitives.

"Ah, to seek, to explore, to bravely venture where no human has ever ventured before," said the man to himself, as he walked up to the door of Aunt Ruth's apartment. He rang the doorbell and was surprised to unexpectedly see the door open in two halves—a top half and a bottom half. The door was split.

"Hello!" said Aunt Ruth, greeting the man. "Sorry for the delay. I was out back, splitting firewood to cozily burn in the fireplace. Would you like to quickly come in for some ice cream with bananas, chocolate and caramel toppings, whipped cream, and nuts?"

"Oh, you mean a banana split? I'd love to delightfully have one!"

Aunt Ruth loved to graciously entertain guests in her split level apartment and was sad when the man said he had to immediately split upon finishing his dessert. She went to the store to prepare for the next visitor.

Lesson 59

Comprehensive Review Part 10

Chapter 27

Rewrite these sentences containing dangling participles or modifiers.

1. Creamy with rich chocolate, Milton was drooling over the cake.

2. Weighing over one thousand pounds, Aunt Ruth was impressed with the large pumpkin at the state fair.

Chapter 28

Select the appropriate words.

3. I think you should give the meatloaf to whomever / whoever you find.

4. George couldn't find the dragon, so he went home to find whomever / whoever it was who had told him about it.

5. Come out, come out, whomever / whoever you are.

Chapter 29

6. I have swam / swum across my bathtub when I was in better shape.

7. I swam / swum across the river this morning.

8. Have you ever bought / buyed an elevator? It has its ups and downs.

Chapter 30

9. There are many / much ways to get tricked by the English language.

10. How much / many oatmeal can you eat in one sitting?

Lesson 60

Comprehensive Review Part 11

Chapter 31

Select the appropriate words.

1. Doris, I found the aardvark. It's sitting on the couch, among / between you and me.

2. Even with the tension of finding herself alone in a room full of hyenas, Marlene was laughing too because she knew that she was among / between friends.

3. Between / Among the seven of us, we managed to carry Aunt Ruth home after her unusual accident involving the handkerchief, the feather, and the Ace of Spades.

4. Itchy Jones received his nickname when, on his first parachute jump, he landed in a field among / between thousands of poison ivy plants.

Chapter 32

5. The students wanted Aunt Ruth to become the principle / principal of the school.

6. Everyone could accept / except that the clown had sprayed water on Jimmy Spivey, accept / except of course for Mrs. Spivey.

7. The principal / principle reason I didn't do well in grade school was because I once accidentally spilled chocolate milk on the principal's / principle's tie.

Chapter 33

8. Wake / Awake me up when Aunt Ruth is done with her speech.

9. Aunt Ruth collects interesting things, e.g. / i.e., TV dinner trays.

10. Aunt Ruth, e.g. / i.e., my great aunt, sure gets a lot of attention these days.

11. I was wokened / wakened when Aunt Ruth fell through the ceiling.

Lesson 61

Comprehensive Review Part 12

Chapter 34

Select the appropriate words.

1. Lawrence's lesser known brother, Clarence of Arabia, spent most of his life in search of the perfect chocolate desert / dessert.

2. Aunt Ruth, how can we ensure / insure that you never vacuum up my dog again?

3. I literally / figuratively gained about 2000 pounds at dinner last night.

Chapter 35

4. It's alright / all right, Georgette; I ate alot / a lot of chocolate mousse too.

5. I think you kids are all right / alright.

6. I like Aunt Ruth a lot / alot.

Chapter 36

Rewrite these sentences containing dropped infinitives.

7. The grapefruit needs peeled.

8. The baklava needs harvested.

9. Aunt Ruth needs dusted.

10. Binky needs bathed.

Lesson 62

Comprehensive Review Part 13

Select the appropriate words.

Chapter 37

1. Jacks / Jack's birthday wish was to go to the zoo with Aunt Ruth.

2. Aunt Ruths / Ruth's lips stuck together after she mistakenly brushed her teeth with super glue.

3. The Robinsons / Robinson's aren't home at the moment.

4. The Joneses / Jones's houseboat sank when Aunt Ruth leaned too far to one side.

Chapter 38

5. The best advise / advice I can give you is to buy all the Aunt Ruth trading cards you can find.

6. I think it's important for kids to advice / advise parents on the latest slang.

7. My mom gave me this advice / advise: Never be advised / adviced by a close relative.

Chapter 39

8. I was affected / effected deeply the day I heard on the news that Aunt Ruth won the international hot dog eating contest.

9. Aunt Ruth is a unique / very unique individual.

10. What were the affects / effects of spending a week on a cruise ship with Aunt Ruth?

11. Read this grammar book and see how it affects / effects you.

Lesson 63

Comprehensive Review Part 14

Chapter 39, Comma Usage

Rewrite the sentences below so that they correctly use commas.

1. Aunt Ruth who was sleepy and grumpy reminded me of two of Snow White's friends.

2. "Wait", said Aunt Ruth, "where are you going?"

3. I need to go to the post office, and then home.

4. Irving from Sleepy Hollow, was terrified of long winter naps.

5. The Headless Horseman, also from Sleepy Hollow was terrified of Irving.

6. "Hey" said the duck "just put it on my bill."

7. Phyllis dreaded her upcoming date, with the Invisible Man as she didn't want to be seen, in public with him.

8. Leonardo da Jones, grocer and distant cousin of the famous artist, told the joke that, made Mona Lisa smile.

Lesson 64

Comprehensive Review Part 15

Select the appropriate words.

Chapter 40

1. When I'm near you, I feel queasy; you must be nauseous / nauseated.

2. I am nauseous / nauseating; I feel awful!

Chapter 41

3. Some people would rather be lead / led, but Aunt Ruth is a natural leader.

4. Don't eat paint chips; they might contain lead / led, which would be harmful to your body.

Chapter 42

5. An interesting phenomena / phenomenon about Aunt Ruth is that she never does quite what one expects of her.

6. Some of the most bizarre phenomena / phenomenon in the known world involve Aunt Ruth and her various relatives.

7. The chief criterion / criteria for selecting Aunt Ruth as president has something to do with her ability to win an arm wrestling contest with the previous president.

Chapter 43

8. In a historic / historical moment, Aunt Ruth went back in time to the D-Day invasion and helped the Allied troops in their ultimate victory.

9. Whether / If you want ketchup or mustard on your hamburger doesn't really matter; we're having chicken instead.

10. Old family historic / historical records indicate that Aunt Ruth consistently improved the grammar of all those around her.

www.ingramcontent.com/pod-product-compliance
Lightning Source LLC
Chambersburg PA
CBHW060518300426
44112CB00017B/2727